THE PARENTAGE AND SIBLINGS OF
ALFRED THOMPSON
BORN IN CONNECTICUT IN 1786

THE PARENTAGE AND SIBLINGS OF
ALFRED THOMPSON
BORN IN CONNECTICUT IN 1786

TOM A. EBELS JR.

Genealogy House
Amherst, Massachusetts

Published 2021 by Genealogy House, a division of White River Press
PO Box 3561, Amherst, Massachusetts 01002 • genealogyhouse.net

ISBN: 978-1-887043-95-3

Cover and book design by Douglas Lufkin, Lufkin Graphic Designs
Norwich, Vermont • www.LufkinGraphics.com

Library of Congress Cataloging-in-Publication Data

Names: Ebels, Tom A., Jr., 1969- author.
Title: The parentage and siblings of Alfred Thompson born in Connecticut in
    1786 / Tom A. Ebels, Jr.
Description: Amherst, Massachusetts : Genealogy House, 2021. | Includes
    bibliographical references and index. | Summary: "According to the
    census of 1850, 1860, and 1870 Alfred Thompson, Sr. was born in
    Connecticut, but no birth records could be located. Tom A. Ebels, Jr.
    examines and analyzes two main sources of information about Alfred
    Thompson, Sr.: The History of Johnson, County, Indiana, published in
    1913 by Elba L. Branigin and the Pension Request files of Alfred and
    Robert Thompson, Jr. He compares, analyzes, and documents his
    findings"-- Provided by publisher.
Identifiers: LCCN 2021012563 | ISBN 9781887043953 (hardcover)
Subjects: LCSH: Thompson family. | Thompson, Alfred, Sr.,
    1786-1872--Family. | United States--Genealogy. | Geauga County
    (Ohio)--Genealogy.
Classification: LCC CS71.T47 2021 | DDC 929.20973--dc23
LC record available at https://lccn.loc.gov/2021012563

DEDICATION

To my grandmother, Gladys Myckowiak Ebels, who wanted to know more about the Thompson and Darby families, and Osca Bemis Daskam and Evabel Robinson TerHune, who left enough breadcrumbs for me to follow.

CONTENTS

I.
INTRODUCTION

According to the U.S. censuses of 1850, 1860, and 1870, Alfred Thompson Sr. was born circa 1786 in Connecticut.[1, 2, 3] However, no birth records could be located. Who, then, are the parents and siblings of Alfred Thompson born in Connecticut, circa 1786? In an attempt to answer these questions, two principal sources were examined: 1) *History of Johnson County, Indiana* by Elba L. Branigin published in 1913 to document the county's history and provide information about its prominent citizens; 2) The pension request files of Alfred and Robert Thompson Jr.

1   1850 U.S. Census, Geauga County, Ohio, population schedule, Auburn Township, p. 516 (penned), p. 258 B (stamped), dwelling 71, family 71, Alfred Thompson family; digital image, ancestry.com, accessed 13 May 2020; from National Archives microfilm M432, roll 682.

2   1860 U.S. Census, Geauga County, Ohio, population schedule, Bainbridge Township, p. 81 (penned), p. 979 (penned), dwelling 691, family 671, Albert [Alfred] Thompson household; digital image, ancestry.com, accessed 13 May 2020; from National Archives microfilm M653, roll 967; Family History Library Film 803967.

3   1870 U.S. Census, Geauga County, Ohio, population schedule, Chester Township, p. 3 (penned), p. 107A (stamped), dwelling 26, family 26, lines 23 and 24, Alfred Thompson family; digital image, ancestry.com, accessed 13 May 2020; from National Archives microfilm M593, roll 1204; Family History Library Film 552703.

Many online family trees utilize Branigin's publication as the basis for determining the descendants of Robert Thompson and Hannah Needham and where the family originated. However, there are several inaccuracies and gaps in his account that lead one to question the reliability of it as the sole source of this information. For *The Parentage and Siblings of Alfred Thompson Born in Connecticut in 1786*, I juxtaposed the *History of Johnson County, Indiana*, with the pension requests of Alfred and Robert Jr., and then compared the data with other sources such as census records, county tax records, War of 1812 payment records, and county histories from Ohio and Wisconsin in order to resolve the conflicts and determine additional lines of study into the Robert Thompson family and their presence in frontier New York, Ohio, Wisconsin, and Michigan. I also examined DNA evidence to help determine lineage.

—Tom A. Ebels Jr.
June 2021

TWO MAIN SOURCES

History of Johnson County, Indiana.

Written by Elba L. Branigin, *History of Johnson County, Indiana* was published in 1913 to document the county's history and provide information about its prominent citizens. The source for the information contained in that text appears to have been Evabel Robinson TerHune, who is a daughter of Cynthia Ellen Burr Robinson, who is the daughter of Alvira Adeline Thompson Burr, who is the daughter of William "Needham" Thompson, who is the son of Robert Thompson. Evabel Robinson married a prominent medical doctor in Johnson County named Rufus Webster TerHune. Consequently, Evabel Robinson appears to have supplied her family history to the publishers.

Pension request files of Alfred and Robert Thompson Jr.

The source of the family information contained in pension request files of Alfred and Robert Thompson Jr. is the correspondence between administrative assistant to Director A. D. Hiller and Osca (Bemis) Daskam. Osca (Bemis) Daskam is a daughter of George

W. Bemis, who is the son of Mary Polly Thompson Bemis, who is the daughter of Robert Thompson.[4,5]

According to the *History of Johnson County, Indiana*, Jasper Thompson is the patriarch of the Thompson family, and Hannah Needham of Ballston Spa, New York, is listed as his marriage partner. Mr. Branigin wrote: "[Jasper Thompson] was a soldier of the Revolution and was severely wounded in the leg. The children of this marriage are: Jasper, Robert, Crowell, Eleanor, Harmer, Needham, and Mary Ann."[6] Alfred is not mentioned among Robert Sr.'s progeny. Additionally, Hannah Needham of Ballston Spa is listed as their mother. The *History of Johnson County, Indiana* also notes that Needham Thompson was born in 1790, in "Ball Town Springs," New York, and served as a drum major in the War of 1812.[7]

In correspondence included in the pension request files of Alfred and Robert Thompson Jr., Osca Daskam wrote to A. D. Hiller, the executive assistant to the administrator for the United States Department of Veterans Affairs in Washington D.C.:

> From my father, George W. Bemis, and from my uncles Jesse Bemis and Loren Bemis, all formerly of Antigo Wisconsin, I have been told that their grandfather, Robert Thompson of New York State, was a soldier in the Revolutionary War. . . . According to a distant relative of mine living in the State of Washington, Revolutionary War soldier

4   Alfred Thompson (Pvt, Capt. Timothy Cornwell's Co., New York Militia, War of 1812), pension file no. S.O. 23821, War of 1812 Pension Files; record group 15, microfilm publication M313, Washington D.C.: National Archives and Records Administration.

5   Robert Thompson Jr. (Pvt., Capt. Timothy Cornwell's Co., New York Militia, War of 1812), pension file no. S.O. 29486, War of 1812 Pension Files; record group 15, microfilm publication M313, Washington D.C.: National Archives and Records Administration.

6   Elba L. Branigin, *History of Johnson County, Indiana*. (Indianapolis, Indiana: B. F. Bowen Company, 1913), pp. 843–844; digital images, online at babel.hathitrust.org, accessed 25 April 2020.

7   Branigin, *History of Johnson County*, p. 843.

Robert Thompson married Hannah Alger. My uncle Loren [sic] was quite certain that her first name was Hannah but was unable to recall her last name. The children of this marriage were: Alfred, Robert, Needham, and Chroel (sons), and Mary Polly, the only daughter. This daughter married Levi Baldwin Bemis, and from their union were born my father and uncles previously named.[8]

On September 14, 1938, A. D. Hiller responded:

Reference is made to your letter in which you request information to Robert Thompson who served from New York in the Revolutionary War, and had five children: Mary, Chroel, Alfred, Robert and Needham. . . . There is no claim for pension or bounty land on file based upon service in the Revolutionary War of any Robert Thompson who served from New York State, found in this office. The records have been found, however, of Alfred and Robert Thompson, brothers, who served in the War of 1812. Their records are furnished herewith, in an effort to aid you in your research.[9]

Four key conflicts between these sources will need to be resolved to determine the parents and siblings of Alfred Thompson born in Connecticut, circa 1786. These conflicts are:

1. Is Jasper Thompson or is Robert Thompson the patriarch of the Thompson family?

8   Pension files of Alfred & Robert Thompson, S.O. 23821 and S.O. 29486.
9   Pension files of Alfred & Robert Thompson, S.O. 23821 and S.O. 29486.

2. Is Hannah Needham of Ballston Spa the family's matriarch—or Hannah Alger?

3. Are the children Jasper, Robert, Crowell, Eleanor, Harmer, Needham, and Mary Ann as indicated in the *History of Johnson County*, or are they Alfred, Chroel, Robert, Needham, and Mary Polly as noted in Osca Daskam's correspondence with the VA?

4. Is Ballston Spa the home of the Thompson family?

Based on the available evidence, it seems that Robert Thompson of Stafford, Connecticut, and Hannah Needham of nearby South Brimfield, Massachusetts, were the parents of Alfred, Robert, Needham, and Chroel (sons), and Mary Polly Thompson.

III.
THE FOUR
MAIN CONFLICTS
BETWEEN THE
SOURCES

The first conflict between the pension file of Robert Thompson Jr. and the *History of Johnson County, Indiana* is whether Jasper Thompson or Robert Thompson is the patriarch of the Thompson family. First, a search was done for Jasper Thompson, and no one named Jasper Thompson could be located. However, according to the Town Records of South Brimfield/Wales, Massachusetts, there is a Jasper Needham who was the father of Hannah Needham of South Brimfield/Wales, Massachusetts, who lived on the Road to Stafford.

Needham family record in Absalom Gardner's 1960 publication,
A Compendium of the History, Genealogy, and Biography of
the Town of Wales and its principal Families and individual
Inhabitants.[10]

Furthermore, the Wales, Massachusetts, records show that Hannah Needham of South Brimfield, Massachusetts, married Robert Thompson of Stafford, Connecticut, on 30 March 1783.

10   Absalom Gardner, *A Compendium of the History, Genealogy, and Biography of the Town of Wales and its principal Families and individual Inhabitants* (n.p.: 1873), Town and City Clerks of Massachusetts. *Massachusetts Vital and Town Records* (Provo, UT: Holbrook Research Institute [Jay and Delene Holbrook Collection]), p. 326; online at ancestry. com, accessed 14 May 2020.

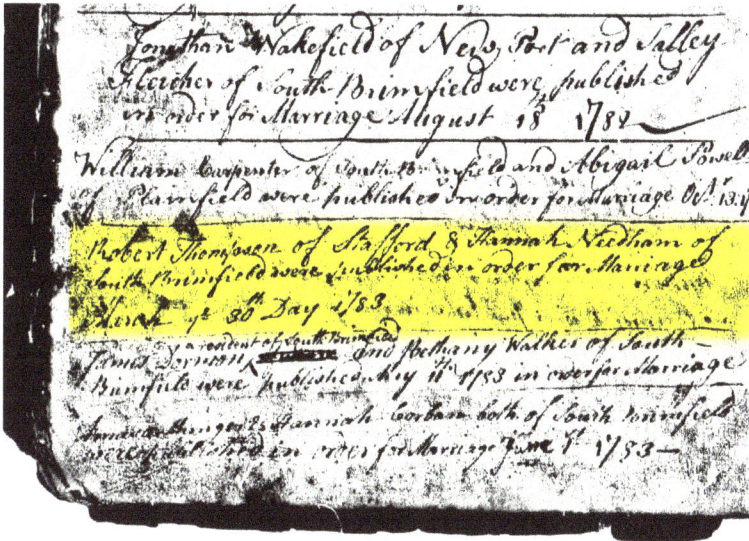

Wales, Massachusetts Marriage Record of Robert Thompson of Stafford Connecticut and Hannah Needham of South Brimfield, Massachusetts.[11]

In addition, a biographical sketch of George W. Bemis states: "Little is known of the family of Polly [Thompson] Bemis, except that she had four brothers whose names were Alfred, Needham, Crowell, and Robert, and their father, Robert Thompson, was in the Revolutionary War...."[12]

---

11   Town and City Clerks of Massachusetts. *Massachusetts Vital and Town Records* (Provo, UT: Holbrook Research Institute [Jay and Delene Holbrook Collection]), marriage of Robert Thompson of Stafford and Hannah Needham of Wales, Massachusetts, 30 March 1783; online at ancestry.com, accessed 14 May 2020.

12   *Commemorative Biographical Record of the Upper Wisconsin: Waupaca, Portage, Wood, Marathon, Lincoln, Oneida, Vilas, Langlade, and Shawano. Biographical Sketches of Present Representative Citizens and of many of the Early Settled Families* (Chicago, Ill.: J. H. Beers & Co., 1895), Sketch of George W. Bemis, pp. 429–430; online at books. google.com, accessed 25 April 2020.

ThruLines™ for Robert Thompson

ThruLines uses Ancestry® trees to suggest that TOM EBELS SR may be related to 15 DNA matches through Robert Thompson.

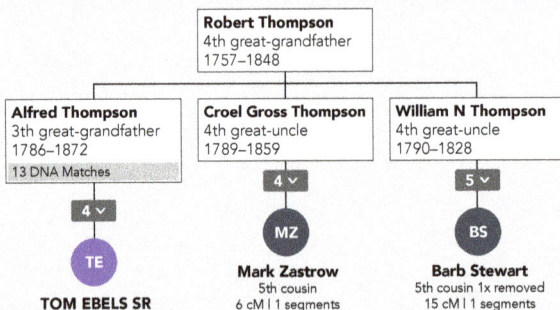

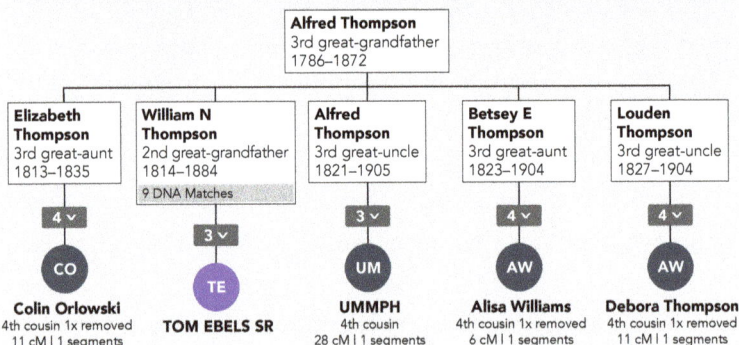

Robert Thompson
4th great-grandfather
1757–1848

Alfred Thompson
3th great-grandfather
1786–1872
13 DNA Matches

4 ⌄

TE
TOM EBELS SR

Croel Gross Thompson
4th great-uncle
1789–1859

4 ⌄

MZ
Mark Zastrow
5th cousin
6 cM | 1 segments

William N Thompson
4th great-uncle
1790–1828

5 ⌄

BS
Barb Stewart
5th cousin 1x removed
15 cM | 1 segments

ThruLines™ for Robert Thompson

ThruLines uses Ancestry® trees to suggest that TOM EBELS SR may be related to 15 DNA matches through Robert Thompson.

Alfred Thompson
3rd great-grandfather
1786–1872

Elizabeth Thompson
3rd great-aunt
1813–1835

4 ⌄

CO
Colin Orlowski
4th cousin 1x removed
11 cM | 1 segments

William N Thompson
2nd great-grandfather
1814–1884
9 DNA Matches

3 ⌄

TE
TOM EBELS SR

Alfred Thompson
3rd great-uncle
1821–1905

3 ⌄

UM
UMMPH
4th cousin
28 cM | 1 segments

Betsey E Thompson
3rd great-aunt
1823–1904

4 ⌄

AW
Alisa Williams
4th cousin 1x removed
6 cM | 1 segments

Louden Thompson
3rd great-uncle
1827–1904

4 ⌄

AW
Debora Thompson
4th cousin 1x removed
11 cM | 1 segments

DNA information from ThruLines™ on AncestryDNA® also shows Robert Thompson as the paternal ancestor of the Thompson family.[13]

The ThruLines on AncestryDNA also appear to indicate that Robert Thompson is the patriarch of the Thompson family. For example, my father, Tom Ebels Sr., has 15 DNA matches with people that trace their ancestry back to Robert Thompson through Alfred (13 matches), Croel (1 match), and William "Needham" Thompson (1 match). Thus, it appears that both the document trail

---

13   AncestryDNA ThruLines, Tom Ebels Sr.; online at ancestry.com, accessed 25 April 2020.

and DNA evidence indicate that Robert Thompson and not Jasper Thompson is the patriarch of the Thompson family of Stafford, Connecticut.

The second conflict between the *History of Johnson County, Indiana* and the pension request files for Robert Thompson Jr. lies with the identity of the matriarch of the Thompson family. The *History of Johnson County* names Hannah Needham of Ballston Spa, New York; the pension files name Hannah Alger as the possible matriarch. As noted above, Hannah Needham of South Brimfield, Massachusetts, married Robert Thompson of Stafford, Connecticut. Also, the birth records from the Town of South Brimfield/Wales show that Hannah Needham was born to Jasper and Deborah (Fuller) Needham on 16 July 1764.

Birth Record of Hannah Needham—Father, Jasper Needham; Mother, Deborah (Fuller) Needham.[14]

---

14   Town and City Clerks of Massachusetts. *Massachusetts Vital and Town Records*, birth of Hannah Needham, 16 July 1764 to Deborah and Jasper Needham, Wales, Massachusetts (Provo, UT: Holbrook Research Institute [Jay and Delene Holbrook]); online at ancestry.com, accessed 25 April 2020.

Needham family record in Absalom Gardner's A Compendium
of the History, Genealogy, and Biography of the Town of
Wales and its principal Families and individual Inhabitants.[15]

The AncestryDNA ThruLines for Tom A. Ebels Sr. again
indicate that Hannah Needham Thompson and not Hannah Alger
is the matriarch of the Thompson family. There are 25 Matches to
Jasper Needham through Naomi Needham (3 matches), Hannah
Needham (9 matches), Mary Polly Needham (4 matches), Ruth
Needham (5 matches), Abner Needham (2 matches), and Daniel
Needham (2 matches).

---

15   Absalom Gardner, *A Compendium of the History, Genealogy, and Biography* . . . Town
and City Clerks of Massachusetts.

ThruLines™ for Jasper Needham

ThruLines uses Ancestry® trees to suggest that TOM EBELS SR may be related to 25 DNA matches through Jasper Needham.

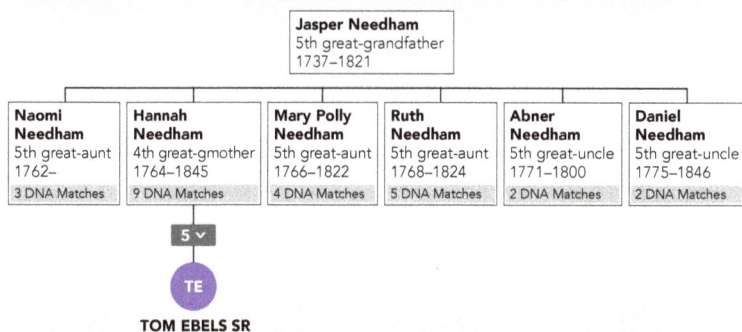

Jasper Needham
5th great-grandfather
1737–1821

Naomi Needham	Hannah Needham	Mary Polly Needham	Ruth Needham	Abner Needham	Daniel Needham
5th great-aunt	4th great-gmother	5th great-aunt	5th great-aunt	5th great-uncle	5th great-uncle
1762–	1764–1845	1766–1822	1768–1824	1771–1800	1775–1846
3 DNA Matches	9 DNA Matches	4 DNA Matches	5 DNA Matches	2 DNA Matches	2 DNA Matches

5 ∨

TE

TOM EBELS SR

Jasper Needham ancestry matches. ThruLines™ at Ancestry.com.[16]

The same number and matches show up for Deborah Fuller as well.

ThruLines™ for Deborah Fuller

ThruLines uses Ancestry® trees to suggest that TOM EBELS SR may be related to 25 DNA matches through Deborah Fuller.

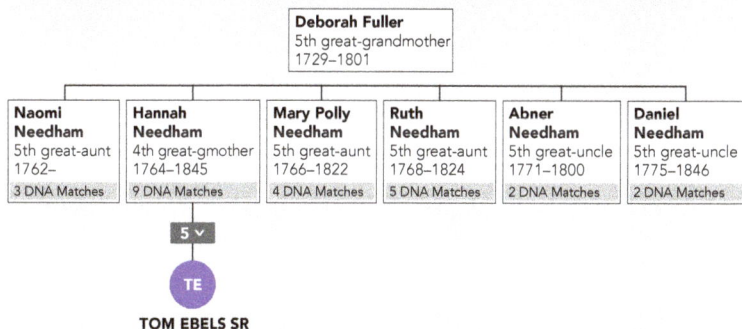

Deborah Fuller
5th great-grandmother
1729–1801

Naomi Needham	Hannah Needham	Mary Polly Needham	Ruth Needham	Abner Needham	Daniel Needham
5th great-aunt	4th great-gmother	5th great-aunt	5th great-aunt	5th great-uncle	5th great-uncle
1762–	1764–1845	1766–1822	1768–1824	1771–1800	1775–1846
3 DNA Matches	9 DNA Matches	4 DNA Matches	5 DNA Matches	2 DNA Matches	2 DNA Matches

5 ∨

TE

TOM EBELS SR

Deborah Fuller ancestry matches. ThruLines™ at Ancestry.com.[17]

16   AncestryDNA ThruLines, Tom Ebels Sr.
17   AncestryDNA ThruLines, Tom Ebels Sr.

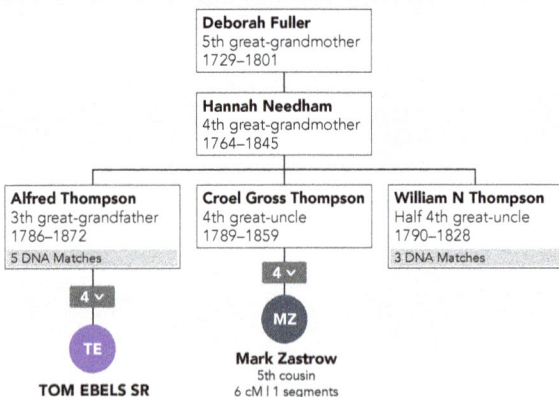

Tom Ebels Sr. possible link to Deborah Fuller. ThruLines™ Ancestry.com,[18]

Interestingly, all the ancestors that have matches are shown on Absalom Gardner's *A Compendium of the History, Genealogy, and Biography of the Town of Wales*. Again, the matches to Hannah go through Alfred Thompson (5), Croel (1), and William "Needham" (3). The DNA evidence combined with the birth and marriage records support the claim that Hannah Needham is the matriarch of the Thompson family as stated in the *History of Johnson County*. However, she did not come from Ballston Spa, New York; rather, she was born and raised in South Brimfield/Wales, Massachusetts.

The third conflict between the *History of Johnson County, Indiana* and the pension request records of Alfred and Robert Jr. is the discrepancy between the children of Robert Thompson and Hannah Needham. The *History of Johnson County* states, "The children of this marriage are: Jasper, Robert, Crowell, Eleanor, Harmer, Needham, and Mary Ann."[19] Branigin also notes that Needham Thompson was born in Ball Town Springs, New York,

---

18 AncestryDNA ThruLines, Tom Ebels Sr.

19 Branigin, *History of Johnson County*, p. 843.

in 1790 and served as a drum major in the War of 1812. However, Alfred is not mentioned at all in the *History of Johnson County, Indiana*.[20]

In contrast, in her correspondence with the U.S. Department of Veterans Affairs in 1938, Osca Daskam writes:

> The children of this marriage were: Alfred, Robert, Needham and Chroel (sons) and Mary Polly, the only daughter. This daughter married Levi Baldwin Bemis and from their union were born my father and uncles previously named.[21]

Searches in the National Archives did reveal that Alfred, Robert, Needham, and Chroel, as well as Mary Polly's husband, Levi Bemis, served in the War of 1812. However, no War of 1812 records could be located for either Jasper or Harmer Thompson.

When one investigates the War Records of 1812, one finds that Alfred, Robert, Needham, and Chroel are very likely brothers as they all served in the same regiment and unit during the War of 1812. First, on 24 March 1874, Robert Thompson Jr. appeared before the Circuit Court of Dunn County, Wisconsin, to claim a pension for his service in the War of 1812:

> He knows of no living comrad[e] of having died some two years ago or more that person's name was Alfred Thompson and a brother of this affiant and served in the same company and he believes was placed on the pension roll for such service as it might only have been a land warrant.[22]

---

20 Branigin, *History of Johnson County*, p. 843.

21 Pension files of Alfred Thompson, S.O. 23821 and Robert Thompson Jr., S.O. 29486.

22 Pension files of Robert Thompson Jr., S.O. 29486.

Although Robert could not prove his claims to the Department of Veterans Affairs at the time of the deposition, his testimony was correct. The index to Compiled Service Records of Volunteer Soldiers Who Served During the War of 1812 from the National Archives shows that Alfred and Robert did serve in the same company. Their pension request files reveal that they also served about the same time.

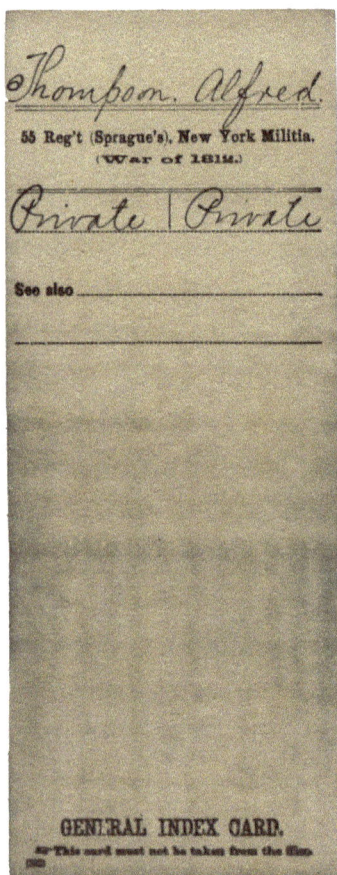

Pension request, Alfred Thompson.[23]

---

23 War of 1812 Service Record Index, Index to Compiled Service Records of Volunteer Soldiers Who Served During the War of 1812, NARA record group 94, M602, Washington D.C.; image 309633740, fold3.com, accessed on 14 May 2020.

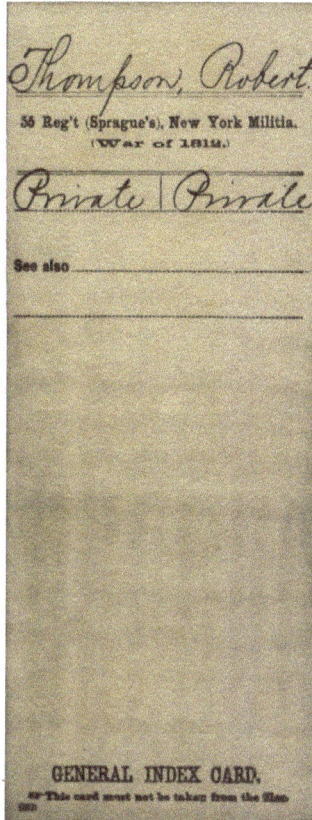

Pension request, Robert Thompson Jr.[24]

Incidentally, Robert Jr. was correct about the Land Patent that Alfred received after he was denied a pension.[25]

---

24 War of 1812 Service Record Index, image 309529145.

25 U.S. Department of the Interior, Bureau of Land Management, General Land Office Records: Document no. 20657; database with images, glorecords.blm.gov, accessed 14 May 2020.

THE UNITED STATES OF AMERICA,

To all to whom these Presents shall come, Greeting:

WHEREAS, In pursuance of the Act of Congress, approved March 3, 1855, entitled "An Act in addition to certain Acts granting Bounty Land to certain Officers and Soldiers who have been engaged in the military service of the United States," there has been deposited in the GENERAL LAND OFFICE, Warrant No. *20,657* for *160* acres, in favor of *Alfred Thompson, private, Captain Cornwell's company New York militia, War 1812,*

with evidence that the same has been duly located upon *the North half of the South-East quarter and the South half of the North-East quarter of Section twenty-nine, in Township thirty-three North of Range twenty-four West, in the district of lands subject to sale at Sunrise City, Minnesota, containing one hundred and sixty acres*

according to the Official Plat of the Survey of said Lands returned to the GENERAL LAND OFFICE by *by the said Alfred Thompson to Patrick McElroy, and by him* the SURVEYOR GENERAL.—*the said Warrant having been duly assigned to Hugh McDonnald, Senior, in whose favor the said tract has been located.*

NOW KNOW YE, That there is therefore granted by the UNITED STATES unto the said *Hugh McDonald, Senior, as assignee as aforesaid, and to his heirs,*

the tract of Land above described: TO HAVE AND TO HOLD the said tract of Land, with the appurtenances thereof, unto the said *Hugh McDonnald, Senior, as assignee as aforesaid, and to his*

heirs and assigns forever.

In testimony whereof, I, *Abraham Lincoln,* PRESIDENT OF THE UNITED STATES OF AMERICA, have caused these Letters to be made Patent, and the SEAL OF THE GENERAL LAND OFFICE to be hereunto affixed.

GIVEN under my hand, at the CITY OF WASHINGTON, the *fifth* day of *September,* in the year of our Lord one thousand eight hundred and *sixty-one*, and of the INDEPENDENCE OF THE UNITED STATES the *eighty-sixth.*

BY THE PRESIDENT: *Abraham Lincoln,*

By *W. O. Stoddard,* Sec'y.

J. N. Granger, Recorder of the General Land Office.

Land Grant, Alfred Thompson.

Robert was also correct about Alfred's approximate date of death of some two or more years. According to Michigan Death Records, Alfred Thompson died on 5 August 1872 in Hopkins, Allegan County, Michigan, at age 86 years, 2 months, and 19 days.

Alfred's parents were not known to the informant.[26] Given the fact that Alfred died in another state before the telephone was invented, Robert probably heard of the death well after the fact.

As indicated in the *History of Johnson County*, Needham did, in fact, serve in the War of 1812 as a drummer. The payroll records of the New York Militia show that Needham Thompson served from 12 October to 14 November 1814.

Payroll record for Needham Thompson.[27]

---

26   Michigan Department of Community Health, Division for Vital Records and Health Statistics, Lansing, Michigan, Death Record for Alfred Thompson Sr., died August 5, 1872; online at ancestry.com, accessed 25 April 2020.

27   New York, War of 1812 Payroll Abstracts for New York State Militia, 1812–1815, Needham Thompson, Drummer, October 12, 1814 to November 14, 1814; digital image, ancestry.com, accessed 25 April 2020.

Likewise, the same group of payroll records shows that Crowell (Chroel) also served in the same regiment and company as Needham did during the War of 1812, although the timeframes are slightly different.

Payroll record for Crowell Thompson.[28]

---

28   New York, War of 1812 Payroll Abstracts for New York State Militia, 1812–1815, Crowell Thompson, May 30, 1814 to June 7, 1814; digital image, ancestry.com, accessed 25 April 2020.

Thompson Family in the U.S. Census

In addition to serving in the same regiment in the War of 1812, the brothers and their families also migrated west together, first to Ellisburg, New York, from Connecticut and Massachusetts; and then to western Ohio. For example, in the 1810 U.S. Census, Alfred Thompson lived in Ellisburg, New York, and was the only member of the Thompson family living there.[29] (See image in Source 9.) However, by the time the 1820 U.S. Census was enumerated, Alfred and Needham Thompson lived in Ellisburg, New York.[30] (See image in Source 10.) In the 1830 U.S. Census, Alfred, Chroel, and Sally Thompson (Needham's widow) lived in Ellisburg, New York (Needham is believed to have died circa 1828).[31] (See image in Source 11.) None of the immediate family members remained in Ellisburg per the 1840 U.S. Census.

1832–1833 *Auswanderung* (Emigration) from Ellisburg, New York, to Western Ohio, and further on to Michigan and Wisconsin

It appears that many of the Thompson family members left Ellisburg between 1832 and 1833, based on the county histories that mention their descendants. According to the book *Pioneer and General History of Geauga County [Ohio], with Sketches of Some of the Pioneers and Prominent Men*:

---

29 1810 U.S. Census, Ellisburg, Jefferson County, New York; roll 28; p. 547; Alfred Thompson, line 5, image 00043; online at ancestry.com, accessed 25 April 2020; from Family History Library Film: 0181382.

30 1820 U.S. Census, Ellisburg, Jefferson County, New York; p. 371; Needham Thompson, line 10; Alfred Thompson, line 13; NARA roll M33_72, image: 205; online at ancestry .com, accessed 25 April 2020.

31 1830 U.S. Census, Ellisburg, Jefferson County, New York; series M19; roll 92; p. 33; Sally Thompson, line 19; Chroel Thompson, line 23; Alfred Thompson, line 27; online at ancestry.com, accessed 25 April 2020; from Family History Library Film: 00171520017152.

Alfred Thompson married in Ellisburgh, New York and came to Auburn with his Family about 1832 and settled on the Miller tract. They had a very large family. Some of their names being—Dorcas, Rhoda, Nelson, Alfred, Louden, Betsey, Mary, Rachel, James, and ten others, whose names we do not know. Mr. Thompson sold his farm to Jesse Garrad about 1858, and left the State for a while, but finally returned and settled in Bainbridge; lived there some time, and we believe went to Michigan and died there several years since. Several of Mr. Thompson's sons resided in Auburn for years but have all gone west. Several of his daughters married in this township, some of whom are now dead, and some are living in other parts.[32]

It is important to note that the information from Alfred's sketch came from the authors of the Geauga County Historical Society and not from Alfred or any of his immediate family members. Thus, it is likely that it is devoid of family information other than that of his immediate family, as the authors may not have known some of the extended family members who settled in Copley, Summit, Ohio, or the "ten others" that "have all gone west."[33]

According to my research, Alfred Sr. had ten children with his first wife, Betsey Benton. He also had two children with his second wife, Phoebe Wilcox, but they did not live beyond infancy. In any case, the year 1833 does appear to be accurate and the names of

32 The Historical Society of Geauga County, Ohio, *The Pioneer and General History of Geauga County [Ohio], with Sketches of Some of the Pioneers and Prominent Men* (Geauga County, Ohio, 1880), pp. 192–193; digital images, books.google.com, accessed 25 April 2020.

33 The Historical Society of Geauga County, Ohio, *The Pioneer and General History of Geauga County [Ohio]*, pp. 192–193.

Alfred's children also are basically correct, and the fact that Alfred Sr. had gone to Michigan and died there is correct. As mentioned above, according to Michigan Death Records, Alfred Thompson died on 5 August 1872 in Hopkins, Allegan County, Michigan, at age 86 years, 2 months, and 19 days. The names of Alfred's parents were not known to the informant.[34] Alfred Thompson Jr. and his sisters Betsey Thompson Calkins and Rachel Thompson Andrews were living in Hopkins, Allegan County, Michigan, at the time of Alfred Sr.'s death, and it is likely he had gone to Michigan to convalesce. According to the censuses of 1850, 1860, and 1870, Alfred Thompson Sr. lived in Geauga County.[35, 36] A "track and trace" of Alfred Sr.'s children follows; it is consistent with the statements in *Pioneer and General History of Geauga County.*

Alfred Thompson Jr.

In 1860, Alfred Thompson Jr. lived in Auburn Township in Geauga County, Ohio.

LAST	FIRST	AGE	SEX	PLACE OF BIRTH	OCCUPATION
Thompson	A [Alfred]	39	Male	New York	Farmer
Thompson	R [Rhoda]	38	Female	New York	None Listed
Thompson	C [Claes]	13	Male	New York	None Listed
Thompson	B [Betsey]	11	Female	Ohio	None Listed
Thompson	M [Malvina]	7	Female	Ohio	None Listed
Thompson	F [Foster]	6	Male	Ohio	None Listed
Thompson	H [Herbert]	3	Male	Ohio	None Listed

---

34   Michigan Department of Community Health, Division for Vital Records and Health Statistics, Lansing, Michigan, Death Record for Alfred Thompson Sr., died August 5, 1872; online at ancestry.com, accessed 25 April 2020.

35   1850 U.S. Census, Geauga County, Ohio, population schedule, Auburn Township, p. 516 (penned), p. 258 B (stamped), dwelling 71, family 71, Alfred Thompson family; digital image, ancestry.com, accessed 13 May 2020; from National Archives microfilm M432, roll 682.

36   1860 U.S. Census, Geauga County, Ohio, population schedule, Bainbridge Township, p. 81 (penned), p. 979 (penned), dwelling 691, family 671, Albert [Alfred] Thompson household; digital image, ancestry.com, accessed 13 May 2020; from National Archives microfilm M653, roll 967; Family History Library Film 803967.

Thompson	D [Delia]	1	Female	Ohio	None Listed
Thompson	Unnamed [Alfred III]	3/12	Male	Ohio	None Listed

Information listed in the 1860 U.S. Census for the Alfred Thompson Jr. family.[37]

However, by 1870, the family had moved to Hopkins Township, Allegan County, Michigan. The same pattern of moving from Geauga County, Ohio, to Michigan, can be observed with all of the Thompson children, except Rhoda and James Thompson who remained in Ohio.

LAST	FIRST	AGE	SEX	PLACE OF BIRTH	OCCUPATION
Thompson	Alfred	49	Male	New York	Farmer
Thompson	Rhoda	48	Female	Ohio	None Listed
Thompson	C H [Claes]	24	Male	Ohio	None Listed
Thompson	Foster	15	Male	Ohio	None Listed
Thompson	Herbert	12	Male	Michigan	None Listed
Thompson	Delia	11	Female	Michigan	None Listed
Thompson	Alfred	10	Male	Michigan	None Listed
Thompson	Ellen	8	Female	Michigan	None Listed
Benson	Fred	9/12	Male	Michigan	None Listed

Information listed in the 1870 U.S. Census for the Alfred Thompson Jr. family.[38]

37   1860 U.S. Census, Geauga County, Ohio, population schedule, Auburn Township, p. 61 (penned), dwelling 499, family 477, Alfred. Thompson [Jr.] household; digital image by subscription, ancestry.com, accessed 9 August 2020; from National Archives microfilm M653, roll 967; Family History Library Film: 803967.

38   1870 U.S. Census, Allegan County, Michigan, population schedule, Hopkins Township, p. 18 (penned), p. 203B (stamped), dwelling 148, family 148, Alfred Thompson [Jr] household; digital image by subscription, ancestry.com, accessed 9 August 2018; from National Archives microfilm M593, roll 660; Family History Library Film: 552159.

Osman & Betsey Thompson Calkins

On 25 January 1844, Betsey Thompson married Osman E. Calkins in Geauga County, Ohio.[39] In 1850, the Osman Calkins and Betsey Thompson family lived in Bainbridge Township, Geauga County, Ohio.

LAST	FIRST	AGE	SEX	PLACE OF BIRTH	OCCUPATION
Calkins	O [Osman]	31	Male	New York	Carpenter
Calkins	Betsey	27	Female	New York	None Listed
Calkins	Byron	5	Male	Ohio	None Listed
Calkins	Henry	3	Male	Ohio	None Listed
Calkins	Alice	1	Female	Ohio	None Listed

Information listed in the 1850 U.S. Census for the Osman Calkins and Betsey Thompson family.[40]

LAST	FIRST	AGE	SEX	PLACE OF BIRTH	OCCUPATION
Calkins	Osmond [Osman]	41	Male	Ohio	Farmer
Calkins	Betsey	37	Female	New York	None Listed
Calkins	Byron	15	Male	Ohio	None Listed
Calkins	Henry	13	Male	Ohio	None Listed
Calkins	Alice	11	Female	Ohio	None Listed
Calkins	Mary	3	Female	Ohio	None Listed

Information listed in the 1860 U.S. Census for the Osman Calkins and Betsey Thompson family.[41] (See image in Source 5.)

However, in 1860, the Osman Calkins and Betsey Thompson family lived in Thetford Township, Genesee County, Michigan, on a parcel adjacent to Betsey's brother William Nelson Thompson.

39　Ohio, County Marriages, 1774–1993, marriage of Betsey Thompson and Osman E. Calkins, 25 January 1844; digital image, ancestry.com, accessed 4 August 2020; Family History Library Film: 000873462.

40　1850 U.S. Census, Geauga County, Ohio, population schedule, Bainbridge, p. 303 (stamped), p. 605 (penned), dwelling 73, family 77, O [Osman] Calkins; digital image, accessed 4 August 2020; National Archives microfilm M432, roll 682.

41　1860 U.S. Census, Genesee County, Michigan, population schedule, Thetford Township, p. 59 (penned), dwelling 1020, family 1014, Osmond Calkins household; digital image by subscription, accessed 9 August 2018; National Archives microfilm M653, roll 544, image 18626; Family History Library Film: 803544.

LAST	FIRST	AGE	SEX	PLACE OF BIRTH	OCCUPATION
Calkins	Osmon E [Osman]	50	Male	New York	Farmer
Calkins	Betsey	46	Female	New York	Keeping House
Calkins	Leila A.	20	Female	Ohio	None Listed
Calkins	May L.	13	Female	Michigan	None Listed

Information listed in the 1870 U.S. Census for the Osman Calkins and Betsey Thompson family.[42]

By 1870, the Osman Calkins and Betsey Thompson family had uprooted and moved to Hopkins Township, Allegan County, Michigan, the same township and county where her brother Alfred Thompson Jr. lived.

John Sloan and Dorcas Thompson

On 21 April 1836, Dorcas Thompson married John Sloan in Geauga County, Ohio.[43] In 1850, John Sloan and Dorcas Thompson Sloan lived in Bainbridge, Geauga County, Ohio.

42 1870 U.S. Census, Allegan County, Michigan, population schedule, Hopkins Township, p. 22 (penned), p. 205B (stamped), dwelling 173, family 175, Osmond E Calkins household; digital image by subscription, ancestry.com, accessed 9 August 2018; National Archives microfilm M593, roll 660; Family History Library Film: 552159.

43 Ohio, County Marriages, 1774–1993 Marriage of Dorcas Thompson and John Sloan, 21 April 1836, Geauga County; digital image by subscription, accessed 9 August 2018; Family History Library Film, 000020255.

LAST	FIRST	AGE	SEX	PLACE OF BIRTH	OCCUPATION
Bettis	Mary	81	Female	Massachusetts	None Listed
Sloane [Sloan]	John	35	Male	Massachusetts	Carpenter
Sloane [Sloan]	Dorcas	33	Female	New York	None Listed
Sloane [Sloan]	Sylvester	13	Male	Ohio	None Listed
Sloane [Sloan]	Adaline	11	Female	Ohio	None Listed
Sloane [Sloan]	John M	6	Male	Ohio	None Listed
Sloane [Sloan]	Eugene	4	Male	Ohio	None Listed
Sloane [Sloan]	Thomas	2	Male	Ohio	None Listed
Mayhew	George	12	Male	Ohio	None Listed

Information listed in the 1850 U.S. Census for the John Sloan and Dorcas Thompson family.[44]

LAST	FIRST	AGE	SEX	PLACE OF BIRTH	OCCUPATION
Sloan	John	44	Male	New York	Merchant
Sloan	[Dorcas]	43	Female	New York	None Listed
Sloan	John M	15	Male	Ohio	Clerk
Sloan	Eugene	13	Male	Ohio	None Listed
Sloan	Thomas	10	Male	Ohio	None Listed
Sloan	Henry	9	Male	Ohio	None Listed
Sloan	Ella	6	Female	Ohio	None Listed
Sloan	May	4	Female	Ohio	None Listed

Information listed in the 1860 U.S. Census for the John Sloan and Dorcas Thompson family.[45]

In 1860, John Sloan and Dorcas Thompson Sloan lived in Vienna, Genesee County, Michigan, close by the William Nelson Thompson and Osman E. Calkins families, who lived in neighboring Thetford Township.

---

44 1850 U.S. Census, Geauga County, Ohio, population schedule, Bainbridge, p. 307B (stamped), line 26, dwelling 143, family 148, John Sloane [Sloan]; digital image, accessed 4 August 2020; National Archives microfilm M432, roll 682.

45 1860 U.S. Census, Genesee County, Michigan, population schedule, Vienna Township, p. 125 (penned), p. 513 (penned), dwelling 983, family 976, John Sloan household; digital image by subscription, accessed 9 August 2018; National Archives microfilm M653, roll 544; image 18626; Family History Library Film: 803544.

Rhoda Thompson and William Harpham

According to the *History of Geauga County,* "[William Harpham] was married in 1841 to Rhoda."[46] The Geauga County marriage records confirm that on 31 December 1840, Rhoda Thompson married William Harpham in Geauga County, Ohio.[47] According to the 1850 and 1860 U.S. Census records, the William Harpham and Rhoda Thompson family lived in Bainbridge, Geauga County, Ohio. William Harpham died in 1878, and Rhoda remained in Geauga County until her death in 1900.[48]

LAST	FIRST	AGE	SEX	PLACE OF BIRTH	OCCUPATION
Harpham	Wm [William]	39	Male	New York	Merchant
Harpham	Rhoda	31	Female	New York	None Listed
Harpham	Betsey T.	13	Male	Ohio	None Listed
Baldwin	Herman	25	Male	Ohio	Clerk

Information listed in the 1850 U.S. Census for the William Harpham and Rhoda Thompson family.[49]

46   The Historical Society of Geauga County, Ohio, *The Pioneer and General History of Geauga County [Ohio],* p. 151; digital images, books.google.com, accessed 25 April 2020.

47   Ohio, County Marriages, 1774–1993, Marriage of Rhoda Thompson and William Harpham, 31 December 1840, Geauga County; digital image by subscription, ancestry.com, accessed 4 August 2020; from Family History Library Film 000020256.

48   Ohio Obituary Index, Rutherford B. Hayes Presidential Library & Museums; ancestry.com, accessed 16 September 2020.

49   1850 U.S. Census, Geauga County, Ohio, population schedule, Bainbridge, p. 304A (stamped), line 8, dwelling 85, family 90, William Harpham family; digital image, ancestry.com, accessed 4 August 2020); from National Archives microfilm M432, roll 682.

LAST	FIRST	AGE	SEX	PLACE OF BIRTH	OCCUPATION
Harpham	Wm [William]	49	Male	New York	Farmer
Harpham	Rhoda	40	Female	New York	None Listed
Harpham	Betty T.	18	Female	Ohio	Teacher
Thompson	Sarah	12	Female	Ohio	None Listed
Andrews	Herman	11	Male	Ohio	None Listed

Information listed in the 1860 U.S. Census for the William Harpham and Rhoda Thompson family.[50]

William "Nelson" Thompson Family

William Nelson Thompson was the oldest son of Alfred Thompson Sr. On official records, he was usually listed as William Nelson Thompson, and it appears he went by his middle name, as both the Geauga Historical Society and a son-in-law referred to him as Nelson. According to the 1850 U.S. Census for the William Nelson Thompson family of Auburn Township of Geauga County, Ohio, the information contained in the book *Pioneer and General History of Geauga County* is correct: William Nelson Thompson married Sarah M. [Marilla] Corbett on 18 January 1845 in Portage County, Ohio, which is where Sarah Marilla was born and lived.[51] (Also, see image in Source 6.)

---

50 1860 U.S. Census, Geauga County, Ohio, population schedule, Bainbridge, p. 878 (stamped), p. 80 (penned), line 32, dwelling 682, family 662, William Harpham family; digital image, ancestry.com, accessed 4 August 2020; from Family History Library Film: 803967.

51 Ohio, County Marriages, 1774–1993, Marriage of William N. Thompson and Sarah M. Corbett, married 18 January 1845, Portage County, Ohio; Family History Film Number 000891360.

LAST	FIRST	AGE	SEX	PLACE OF BIRTH	OCCUPATION
Thompson	Wm [William]	36	Male	New York	Farmer
Thompson	M. [Marilla]	26	Female	Ohio	None Listed
Thompson	Rosalia	4	Female	Ohio	None Listed
Thompson	Albert [Adelbert]	3	Male	Ohio	None Listed
Thompson	Sarah	2	Female	Ohio	None Listed
Thompson	Corwin	1	Male	Ohio	None Listed
Sutton	Harriet	28	Female	Ohio	None Listed

Information listed in the 1850 U.S. Census for the William Nelson Thompson family.[52] (Also, see image in Source 1.)

In 1850, the Thompson family lived in Auburn Township, County of Geauga, Ohio. The census was enumerated on 11 September 1850. (See image of the census page in Source 1.) It shows William, age 36; M. [Marilla], age 26; Rosalia, age 4; Albert, age 3; Sarah, age 2; Corwin, age 1; and Harriet Sutton, age 28. William is listed as being born in New York, and the rest of the family is shown as being born in Ohio.

"M. Thompson" is short for Marilla Thompson. Marilla Thompson's full name was Sarah Marilla Corbett Thompson. Many online trees list Sarah Marilla Corbett as "Amelia Cobex." The error stems from an incorrect transcription of Marilla Corbett found in her son Adelbert Thompson's death record.[53] It is not the purpose of this paper to prove, but listing "Amelia Cobex" as the mother is a common mistake in many online trees for the Thompson family that needs to be rectified.

Although no birth or death records could be located for Sarah Marilla Corbett Thompson, the death records of two of her children and her father's will provide the evidence of her married and

52   1850 U.S. Census, Geauga County, Ohio, population schedule, Auburn, p. 260 (stamped), p. 80 (penned), dwelling 94, family 94, Wm [William] Thompson; digital image, ancestry.com, accessed 4 August 2018; from National Archives microfilm M432, roll 682.

53   "Michigan Deaths and Burials, 1800–1995," Adelbert Thompson death date 15 March 1889; database, FamilySearch.org, 26 March 2020, accessed July 29. 2020; index based on data collected by the Genealogical Society of Utah, Salt Lake City.

maiden names. First, Rhoda Thompson Darby's death certificate indicates that her mother's name was Marilla Corbelt [Corbett]; Victor Darby, Rhoda Darby's son (incorrectly listed as her husband on the death certificate) and Marilla Thompson's grandson, was the informant.[54] (See image in Source 2.) Second, the death certificate of William Thompson II offers evidence of Sarah Marilla Corbett's name. William Thompson II's mother is listed as Sarah Corbett. Harriet Thompson Trumbull, sister of William II and Rhoda, was the informant.[55] (See image in Source 3.) Third, Nathaniel Corbett III of Portage County, Ohio, lists Sarah Marilla Thompson in his will. Mostly likely, Sarah Marilla went by her middle name, because her mother's name was also Sarah as evidenced in Nathaniel Corbett III's will of 1857. (See images in Sources 4-1, 4-2, and 4-3 for Nathaniel Corbett's will.)[56] In addition, Clyde H. Corbett mentions Sarah Marilla in his *Genealogy of the Descendants of Robert Corbett*: "Sarah Marilla [Corbett]. b. about 1825, m. Jan 18, 1845. William N. Thompson; migrated to Michigan. Had a Large family. Lost account of."[57]

The 1860 U.S. Census shows how the family of William Nelson Thompson changed in the ten-year span between 1850 and 1860. (See Source 5 for the full image.) Sarah appears to have died between Rhoda's birth in February of 1856 and William's remarriage to Lucy Keyes in September of 1859.[58] (See Source 8.)

---

54 Michigan Death Records 1867–1950, Department of State—Division of Vital Statistics, Register Number 1741, Rhoda Ann Darby; digital image by subscription, ancestry.com, accessed 9 August 2018.

55 Michigan Death Records 1867–1950, Department of State—Division of Vital Statistics, Register Number 29 3950, Wm [William]Thompson [II]; digital image by subscription, ancestry.com, accessed 9 August 2018.

56 Ohio, Wills and Probate Records, 1786–1998, Will Records, 1823–1918; Probate Place: Portage, Ohio, Will of Nathaniel Corbett; digital image by subscription, ancestry.com., accessed 9 August 2018.

57 Clyde Corbett, *Genealogy of the Descendants of Robert Corbett* (Canton Ohio: Canton Printing Company, 1947), p. 18.

58 "Ohio, County Marriages, 1789-2016," database with images, FamilySearch (https://familysearch.org/ark:/61903/1:1:XZCG-44Y : 8 March 2021), William N. Thompson and Lucy J. Keyes, 05 Sep 1859; citing Marriage, Geauga, Ohio, United States, pg 333, Franklin County Genealogical & Historical Society, Columbus; FHL microfilm.

LAST	FIRST	AGE	SEX	PLACE OF BIRTH	OCCUPATION
Thompson	William N.	45	Male	New York	Farmer
Thompson	Lucy	30	Female	Ohio	None Listed
Thompson	Adelbert	13	Male	Ohio	None Listed
Thompson	Corwin	10	Male	Ohio	None Listed
Thompson	William	9	Male	Ohio	None Listed
Thompson	Melvin	8	Male	Ohio	None Listed
Thompson	Ella	7	Female	Ohio	None Listed
Thompson	Rhoda	3	Female	Ohio	None Listed

Information listed in the 1860 U.S. Census for the William Nelson Thompson family.[59] (See image in Source 5.)

In addition, by 1860, the Thompson family had moved from Geauga County, Ohio, to Thetford Township in Genesee County, Michigan. As mentioned above, William Nelson's sister Betsey Thompson Calkins lived on the adjacent parcel of land in 1860.

1859 Plat Map of Thetford Township, Genesee County, Michigan.[60]

---

59   1860 U.S. Census, Genesee County, Michigan, population schedule, Thetford Township, p. 519 (penned), dwelling 1018, family 1012, William N. Thompson household; digital image by subscription, ancestry.com, accessed 9 August 2018); from National Archives microfilm M653, roll 544; image: 18626; Family History Library Film: 803544.

60   Library of Congress, loc.gov/item/2011588008/, accessed August 2018.

The 1870 U.S. Census for William N. Thompson shows that the family had grown and that they had moved from Thetford Township in Genesee County to Flushing Township (also in Genesee County, Michigan).

LAST	FIRST	AGE	SEX	PLACE OF BIRTH	OCCUPATION
Thompson	William	56	Male	New York	Farmer
Thompson	Lizzie [Lucy]	60	Female	Ohio	Keeping House
Thompson	Adelbert	23	Male	Ohio	Farm Laborer
Thompson	Sarah	22	Female	Ohio	At Home
Thompson	Corwin	20	Male	Ohio	Farm Laborer
Thompson	William	19	Male	Ohio	At Home
Thompson	Ella	17	Female	Michigan	At Home
Thompson	Harriet	14	Female	Michigan	At School
Thompson	Rhoda	13	Female	Michigan	At School
Thompson	Delia	8	Female	Michigan	At School
Thompson	Eunice	6	Female	Michigan	At School
Thompson	Willard	3	Male	Michigan	None Listed

Information as listed in the 1870 U.S. Census for the William Nelson Thompson family.[61] (See image in Source 7.)

---

61 1870 U.S. Census, Genesee County, Michigan, population schedule, Flushing Township, p. 17 (penned), p. 210 (stamped), dwelling 123, family 119, William Thompson household; digital image by subscription, ancestry.com, accessed 9 August 2018; from National Archives microfilm M593, roll 671; Family History Library Film: 552170.

Louden Thompson

In 1850, the Louden Thompson family lived in Auburn Township, County of Geauga, Ohio. The census was enumerated on 4 September 1850, and listed Louden, age 26; Lovina, age 21; G [George], age 3; and H [Henry], age 1.

LAST	FIRST	AGE	SEX	PLACE OF BIRTH	OCCUPATION
Thompson	L [Louden]	26	Male	New York	Farmer
Thompson	Lovina	21	Female	New York	None Listed
Thompson	G [George]	3	Male	New York	None Listed
Thompson	H [Henry]	1	Male	New York	None Listed

Information listed in the 1850 U.S. Census for the Louden Thompson family.[62] (See image in Source 12.)

LAST	FIRST	AGE	SEX	PLACE OF BIRTH	OCCUPATION
Thompson	Londen [Louden]	34	Male	New York	Farmer
Thompson	Lomira [Lovina]	32	Female	New York	None Listed
Thompson	G [George]	13	Male	New York	None Listed
Thompson	H [Henry]	11	Male	New York	None Listed

Information listed in the 1860 Census for the Louden Thompson family.[63]

By 1860, the census showed the Louden Thompson family as living in Arbela Township, County of Tuscola, Michigan. It listed Louden as age 34; Lovina, age 32; George, age 13; and Henry, age 11. The entire family was born in New York according to this census.

---

62 1850 U.S. Census, Geauga County, Ohio, population schedule, Auburn, p. 261 (stamped), dwelling 117, family 118, Louden Thompson; digital image, ancestry.com, accessed 4 August 2018; from National Archives microfilm M432, roll 682.

63 1860 U.S. Census, Tuscola County, Michigan, population schedule, Arbela Township, p. 82 (penned), dwelling 696, family 696, Londen [Louden] Thompson household; digital image by subscription, ancestry.com, accessed 9 August 2020; from Family History Library Film: 803562.

Rachel Thompson and Eleazer Andrews

Rachel Thompson and Eleazer Andrews were married on 17 April 1853 in Geauga County, Ohio.[64] Although they could not be located in the 1850 U.S. Census, the 1860 census indicates that Eleazer Andrews and Rachel Thompson are neighbors to Louden Thompson in Arbela Township, Tuscola County, Michigan.

LAST	FIRST	AGE	SEX	PLACE OF BIRTH	OCCUPATION
Andrews	Eleazer	47	Male	New York	Farmer
Andrews	Rachel	32	Female	New York	Servant
Andrews	Eldoras	4	Male	Michigan	None Listed

Information listed in the 1860 U.S. Census for the Eleazer Andrews and Rachel Thompson family.[65]

By 1870, the Andrews family lives in Hopkins Township, Allegan County, Michigan, along with Alfred Jr. and Betsey Thompson Calkins.

LAST	FIRST	AGE	SEX	PLACE OF BIRTH	OCCUPATION
Andrews	Eleazer	57	Male	New York	Farmer
Andrews	Rachel	41	Female	New York	Servant
Andrews	Eldorus	14	Male	Michigan	None Listed
Andrews	Charles	7	Male	Michigan	None Listed

Information listed in the 1870 U.S. Census for the Eleazer Andrews and Rachel Thompson family.[66]

---

64 Ohio, County Marriages, 1774–1993, Rachel Thompson and Eleazer Andrews, 17 April 1853, Geauga County, Ohio; digital image by subscription, ancestry.com, accessed 9 August 2020.

65 1860 U.S. Census, Tuscola County, Michigan, population schedule, Arbela Township, p. 82 (penned), dwelling 692, family 692, Eleazar Andrews household; digital image by subscription, ancestry.com, accessed 9 August 2020; from Family History Library Film: 803562.

66 1870 U.S. Census, Allegan County, Michigan, population schedule, Hopkins Township, p. 11 (penned), p. 200 (stamped), dwelling 88, family 89, Eleazar Andrews household; digital image by subscription, ancestry.com, accessed 9 August 2020; from National Archives microfilm M593, roll 660; Family History Library Film: 552159.

James Thompson

In 1850, James Thompson lived with Alfred Sr. and his stepmother, Phoebe, in Auburn Township, Geauga County, Ohio.[67] In 1860, James was living with Alfred Sr. and his stepmother, Phoebe, in Bainbridge Township, Geauga County, Ohio.[68] By 1870, James Thompson was married and living in Chester Township, Geauga County, Ohio.[69]

Other county histories containing information on Chroel Thompson, Needham Thompson's surviving family members, Mary Polly (Thompson) Bemis, as well as those of their descendants, tell a similar story of migrating from Ellisburg to Ohio and then to either Michigan or Wisconsin. For example, Chroel Thompson Sr. moved from Ellisburg, New York (as per the 1830 U.S. Census);[70] Copley, Summit, Ohio (as per the 1840 U.S. Census);[71] and finally Hustisford, Dodge, Wisconsin (as per the 1850 U.S. Census).[72] An 1892 book titled *Biographical History of LaCrosse, Monroe, and Juneau Counties, Wisconsin . . .* also indicates that Chroel and his descendants followed this path:

---

67   1850 U.S. Census, Geauga County, Ohio, population schedule, Auburn, p. 258 (stamped), dwelling 71, family 71, James Thompson inferred son of Alfred Thompson; digital image, ancestry.com, accessed 4 August 2018; from National Archives microfilm M432, roll 682.

68   1860 U.S. Census, Geauga County, Ohio, population schedule, Bainbridge, p. 979 (penned), p. 81 (penned), line 32, dwelling 691, family 671, James Thompson in Alfred Thompson Sr. family; digital image, ancestry.com, accessed 4 August 2020; from Family History Library Film: 803967.

69   1870 U.S. Census, Geauga County, Michigan, population schedule, Chester Township, p. 10 (penned), p. 200 (stamped), dwelling 97, family 95, James Thompson household; digital image by subscription, ancestry.com, accessed 9 August 2020; from National Archives microfilm M593, roll 1204; Family History Library Film: 552703.

70   1830 U.S. Census, Ellisburg, Jefferson, New York, series M19, roll 92, p. 33; Chroel Thompson, line 23; from Family History Library Film: 0017152.

71   1840 U.S. Census, Copley, Summit, Ohio, Chroel Thompson, line 6, roll: 428, p. 243; online at ancestry.com, accessed 25 April 2020; from Family History Library Film: 0020177.

72   1850 U.S. Census, Hustisford, Dodge, Wisconsin, population schedule, p. 212B (stamped), p. 424 (penned), dwelling 17, family 17, Chroel Thompson, line 37; NARA Microfilm publications roll M432_996, image: 419; online at ancestry.com, accessed 25 April 2020.

Benjamin B. Thompson and his brother, Chroel G. Thompson [Jr.], of Elroy are numbered among the Pioneers of Juneau County. The former was born in Jefferson County, New York, in January 1831, and the latter, in Ohio, November 18, 1833 . . . The Father of our subjects Chroel G. Thompson [Sr.] married Catherine Bemis, a Native of Vermont, and in 1833 they removed to Ohio and located in Geauga county; there they resided until 1844 when they came to Wisconsin, which was then a territory; they settled in Dodge county on Government land, occupying the present site of Hustisford; Mr. Thompson assisted in the organization of the town. In 1854, the parents and two sons came to Junea County. . . .[73]

An earlier book, *The History of Dodge County, Wisconsin* . . . , published in 1880, confirms: "During the Spring and Summer of 1845 . . . Croel [Chroel] Thompson, settled on the east side of the river [in Hustisford Township, Dodge County, Wisconsin]."[74]

According to Elba Branigin's *History of Johnson County, Indiana*, following Needham's death, his descendants also moved to Ohio from Ellisburg, New York. "He [Harry Burr] was married to Alvira Adeline Thompson of Ellisburg, [28 February 1833]. He moved that same year to Copley, Ohio. . . . Needham and Sally (Holley) Thompson were the parents of Owen, Ora, William, Alvira Adeline, Cynthia, Alzina Emmeline, and Sally Anne."[75] Sally Hawley Thompson, Needham's widow, also made the move from Ellisburg,

---

73 *Biographical History of LaCrosse, Monroe, and Juneau Counties, Wisconsin* (Chicago, Ill.: The Lewis Publishing Company, 1892), pp. 889–890; Murphy Library database with images, digitalcollections.uwlax.edu/, accessed 24 July 2020.

74 *The History of Dodge County, Wisconsin* (Chicago, Illinois, Western Historical Company, 1880), p. 410; online at books.google.com, accessed 25 April 2020.

75 Branigin, *History of Johnson County, Indiana*, p. 843.

New York to Copley, Summit, Ohio. She married Almerin Fuller in Summit County, Ohio on 15 September 1840.[76] After Almerin Fuller died she moved to Wells, Monroe County, Wisconsin to live with her daughter Sarah and son-in-law Richard DeWitt.[77]

The lives and migration paths of Levi and Polly (Thompson) Bemis are described in the biographies of their sons, George W. Bemis, Lorin Bemis, and Jesse Bemis contained in *Commemorative Biographical Record of the Upper Wisconsin: Waupaca, Portage, Wood, Marathon, Lincoln, Oneida, Vilas, Langlade, and Shawano. Biographical Sketches of Present Representative Citizens and of many of the Early Settled Families.*[78]

According to the book, George W. Bemis ". . . was born in Auburn, Geauga Co., Ohio, [5] March 1840 and is the son of Levi and Polly (Thompson) Bemis." Also: "In 1833, Levi Bemis went to Ohio, and about 1843, pushed on to Illinois with a team locating in Kane County. He came to Wisconsin in 1846, settled on a piece of Land near OshKosh, and here his wife Polly died within 3 weeks of arrival."

The biographies of Lorin B. Bemis and Jesse Bemis vary a bit from their brother, George, in that they omit the Ohio stage in the migration; however, they are basically in agreement. Beginning in 1830, census records for their father, Levi Bemis, clearly show the migration path from Ellisburg, New York, to Auburn, Geauga County, Ohio, and then on to Wisconsin in 1850 and 1860. Per the 1830 U.S. Census, Levi Bemis lived in Ellisburg, New York;[79]

---

76   Ohio, County Marriages, 1774–1993, Summit County, Ohio, Marriage Records, 1840–1980, roll 13, Summit County Court of Common Pleas— Probate Division, Akron, Ohio; volume number or range of dates: vol. A–C 1840–1865; roll: 0309S, Almerin Fuller to Sally Hawley; online at ancestry.com, accessed 25 April 2020).

77   1880 U.S. Census, population schedule, Wells, Monroe, Wisconsin; Enumeration District 036, p. 13 (penned), p. 178A (stamped), family 122, Sally Fuller (mother-in-law), roll: 1439; online at ancestry.com, accessed 25 April 2020.

78   *Commemorative Biographical Record of the Upper Wisconsin . . .*, pp. 429–430.

79   1830 U.S. Census, Ellisburg, Jefferson, New York; series M19, roll 92, p. 33; Levi Bemis, line 25; online at ancestry.com, accessed 25 April 2020; from Family History Library Film: 00171520017152.

in 1840, the U.S. Census finds him in Auburn, Geauga County, Ohio;[80] in 1850, he lived in Vinland Township, Winnebago County, Wisconsin;[81] and in the 1860 census he is listed in Greenville Township, Outagamie County, Wisconsin.[82]

Following the War of 1812, Robert Jr. appears to have gone off in a different direction from Alfred, Chroel, Needham's surviving family members, and Polly (Thompson) Bemis. Namely, he appears to have traveled north with Robert Sr. to Upper Canada before moving to Michigan, circa 1850, and on to Wisconsin in 1860, where he died in 1877.

There were no records found for Robert Sr. following the family's departure from Stafford, Connecticut, around 1788. However, there are some clues in the county history as to his fate. For example, George W. Bemis's biography reads: ". . . Polly [Thompson] Bemis had four brothers whose names were Alfred, Needham, Crowell, and Robert, and their father Robert [Sr.] was in the Revolutionary War, was one of Washington's life guards, and after the struggle [he] went to Canada, where he died."[83] As previously mentioned, it appears that Robert Jr. went to Canada during this same period. The *History of Johnson County* also mentions Robert Sr.'s Revolutionary War service: " . . . Jasper [Robert Sr.] of Ballston Spa, New York . . . was a soldier of the Revolution and was severely wounded in the leg."[84] In her correspondence with the Department of Veterans Affairs, Robert Sr.'s great-granddaughter

---

80   1840 U.S. Census, Auburn, Geauga, Ohio; Levi Bemis, line 18, roll 395, p. 142; online at ancestry.com, accessed 25 April 2020; from Family History Library Film: 0020165.

81   1850 U.S. Census, Vinland, Winnebago, Wisconsin; p. 499A (stamped), p. 997 (penned), dwelling 688, family 703; Levi Bemis, NARA Microfilm Publications: M432 roll 1009, image 524; online at ancestry.com, accessed 25 April 2020.

82   1860 U.S. Census, Greenville, Outagamie, Wisconsin; p. 508 (penned), p. 98 (penned), dwelling 712, family 684; Levi Bemis, NARA Microfilm Publications: M653 roll 1424; online at ancestry.com, accessed 25 April 2020; from Family History Library Film: 805424.

83   *Commemorative Biographical Record of the Upper Wisconsin . . .*, pp. 429–430.

84   Branigin, *History of Johnson County, Indiana*, p. 843.

Osca Daskam also mentions his Revolutionary War service. On 10 August 1938 she wrote:

> Will you please advise me on the Revolutionary Soldier Robert Thompson, 18 years old, we the descendants have very little except family tradition handed to us by our fathers who were his grandsons. We've been told by them that Robert Thompson was 18 years old when he enlisted in the Rev. in the State of New York and that he was taken prisoner and taken to England later exchanged and again entered the service and stayed until the end of the War. When he married, and to whom, no one seems to know.[85]

Although the details of Robert Sr.'s Revolutionary War service vary, it does seem likely that he did serve in the war, which is a topic ripe for future study.

---

85   Pension Files of Robert Thompson Jr., S.O. 29486.

IV.
CONCLUSIONS

Relative to Conflict 1: The father of Alfred Thompson of Stafford, Connecticut, is Robert Thompson Sr. of Stafford, Connecticut.

Relative to Conflict 2: The mother of Alfred Thompson of Stafford, Connecticut, is Hannah Needham, the daughter of Jasper Needham & Deborah Fuller of Wales/South Brimfield, Massachusetts.

Relative to Conflict 3: The confirmed children of Robert Thompson Sr. of Stafford, Connecticut, and Hannah Needham of Wales/South Brimfield, Massachusetts, are Alfred, Robert Jr., Needham, and Chroel (sons), and Mary Polly (daughter).

Conflict 4: Alfred, Robert Jr., Needham, and Chroel all served in the same regiment during the War of 1812, and all but Robert Jr. lived in Ellisburg at the time; and all migrated to western Ohio between 1832 and 1833, except Needham who passed away, circa 1828, and Robert Jr. who went to Canada before he migrated to Michigan, circa 1850, and then to Wisconsin, circa 1860.

Based on the above research, additional research will be conducted into the following topics:

1. The unconfirmed Thompson children mentioned in the *History of Johnson County, Indiana*, namely, Jasper, Eleanor, and Harmer.

2. Robert Thompson Sr.'s birth, his parents, and possible death in Canada need further investigation.

3. Robert Thompson Sr.'s Revolutionary War service. While it appears likely that Robert Thompson Sr. did serve in the Revolutionary War based on the consistent references in the county histories and the War of 1812 pension request correspondence for Robert Jr., more investigation is necessary.

4. Hannah Needham Thompson's death date and place of death are unknown and in need of further investigation.

5. Possible places of residence mentioned in the *History of Johnson County, Indiana*, namely, Ballston Spa/ Ball Town Springs. It is possible that the Thompson family did live in Ballston Spa and Ball Town Springs; however, more investigation into the local level data is necessary to determine this.

SOURCES

1.   1850 U.S. Census, recording William Thompson and Alfred Thompson Jr.[86]

86   1850 U.S. Census, Geauga County, Ohio, population schedule, Auburn, p. 260 (stamped), p. 80 (penned), dwelling 94, family 94, Wm [William] Thompson; digital image, ancestry.com, accessed 4 August 2018; from National Archives microfilm M432, roll 682.

2.   Rhoda Thompson Darby, Death Certificate.

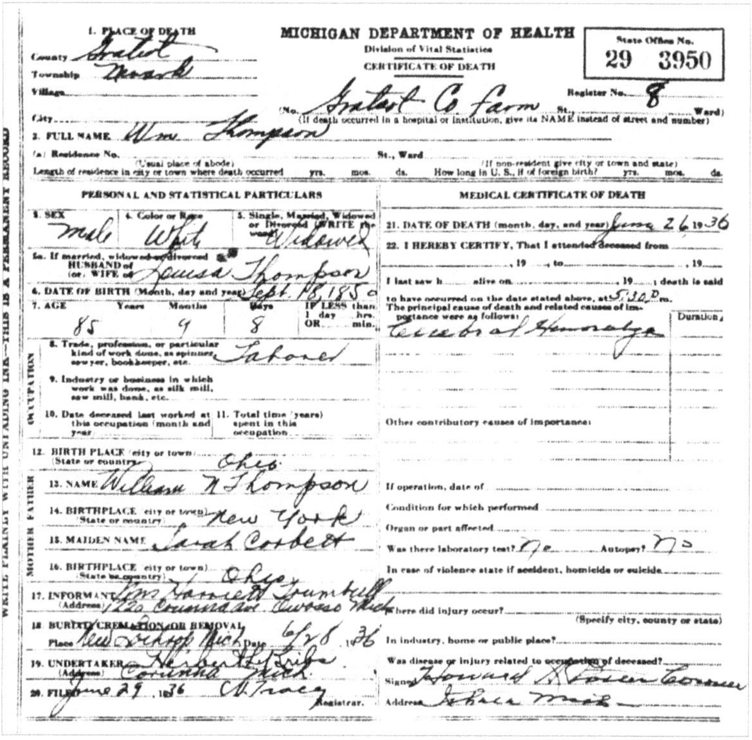

WRITE PLAINLY WITH UNFADING INK—THIS IS A PERMANENT RECORD

MICHIGAN DEPARTMENT OF HEALTH
Division of Vital Statistics
CERTIFICATE OF DEATH

State Office No. 29 3950

1. PLACE OF DEATH
County Gratiot
Township Newark
Village
City
(No. Gratiot Co Farm St., Ward)
(If death occurred in a hospital or institution, give its NAME instead of street and number)
Register No. 8

2. FULL NAME Wm Thompson
(a) Residence No. St., Ward
(Usual place of abode) (If non-resident give city or town and state)
Length of residence in city or town where death occurred yrs. mos. ds. How long in U. S., if of foreign birth? yrs. mos. ds.

PERSONAL AND STATISTICAL PARTICULARS

3. SEX Male
4. Color or Race White
5. Single, Married, Widowed or Divorced (WRITE the word) Widowed
5a. If married, widowed or divorced HUSBAND of (or) WIFE of Louisa Thompson
6. DATE OF BIRTH (Month, day and year) Sept. 18, 1850
7. AGE Years 85 Months 9 Days 8 IF LESS than 1 day hrs. OR min.
8. Trade, profession, or particular kind of work done, as spinner, sawyer, bookkeeper, etc. Laborer
9. Industry or business in which work was done, as silk mill, saw mill, bank, etc.
10. Date deceased last worked at this occupation (month and year)
11. Total time (years) spent in this occupation
12. BIRTH PLACE (city or town) (State or country) Ohio

FATHER
13. NAME William N Thompson
14. BIRTHPLACE (city or town) (State or country) New York

MOTHER
15. MAIDEN NAME Sarah Corbett
16. BIRTHPLACE (city or town) (State or country) Ohio

17. INFORMANT Mrs Harriett Trumbull
(Address) 1220 Corunna Ave. Owosso Mich
18. BURIAL, CREMATION, OR REMOVAL
Place New Lothrop Mich. Date 6/28 1936
19. UNDERTAKER Herbert H. Kribs
(Address) Corunna Mich.
20. FILED June 29, 1936 A. Tracy Registrar.

MEDICAL CERTIFICATE OF DEATH

21. DATE OF DEATH (month, day, and year) June 26 1936
22. I HEREBY CERTIFY, That I attended deceased from , 19 , to , 19
I last saw h alive on 19 ; death is said to have occurred on the date stated above, at 5:30 P m.
The principal cause of death and related causes of importance were as follows: Cerebral Hemorrhage
Duration
Other contributory causes of importance:
If operation, date of
Condition for which performed
Organ or part affected
Was there laboratory test? No Autopsy? No
In case of violence state if accident, homicide or suicide
Where did injury occur?
(Specify city, county or state)
In industry, home or public place?
Was disease or injury related to occupation of deceased?
Signed Howard H. Power Coroner
Address Ithaca Mich

3. William Thompson II, Death Certificate.

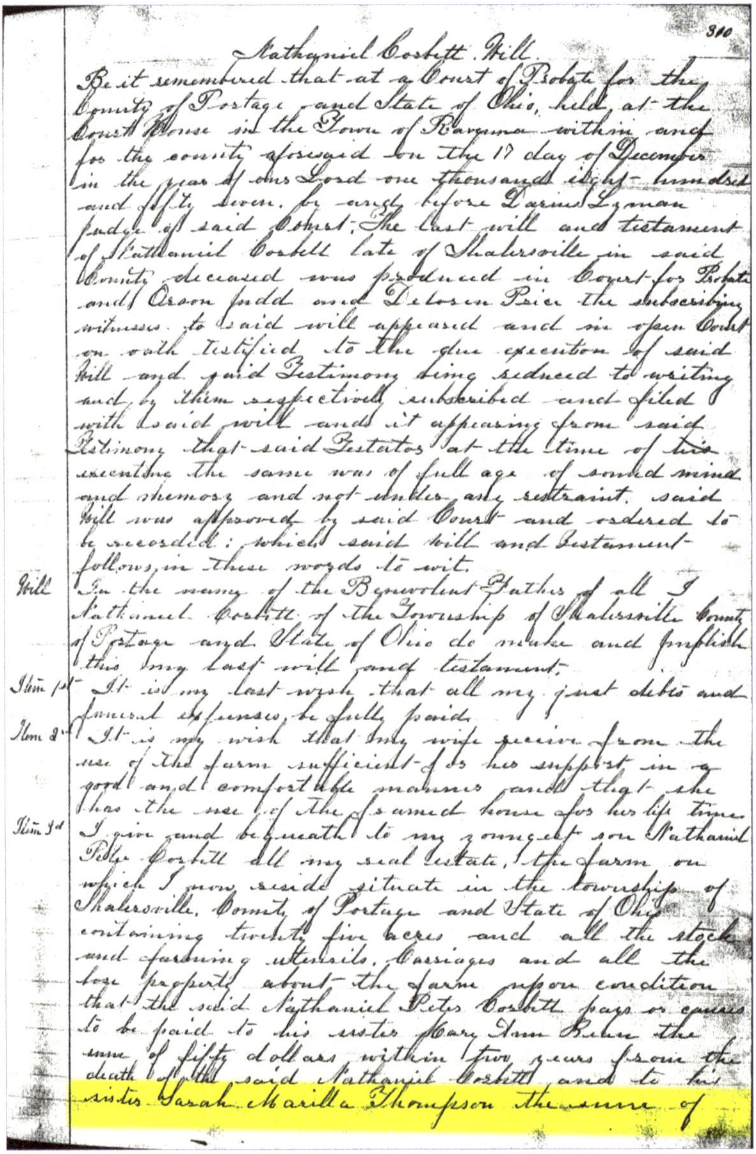

Nathaniel Corbett Will. 310

Be it remembered that at a Court of Probate for the County of Portage and State of Ohio, held at the Court House in the Town of Ravenna within and for the county aforesaid on the 17 day of December in the year of our Lord one thousand eight hundred and fifty seven, personally before Darius Lyman Judge of said Court; The last will and testament of Nathaniel Corbett late of Shalersville in said County deceased was produced in Court for Probate and Orson Judd and Deloson Price the subscribing witnesses to said will appeared and in open Court on oath testified to the due execution of said Will and said Testimony being reduced to writing and by them respectively subscribed and filed with said will and it appearing from said Testimony that said Testator at the time of his executing the same was of full age of sound mind and memory and not under any restraint, said Will was approved by said Court and ordered to be recorded: which said Will and Testament follows, in these words to wit.

Will In the name of the Benevolent Father of all I Nathaniel Corbett of the Township of Shalersville County of Portage and State of Ohio do make and publish this my last will and testament;

Item 1st It is my last wish that all my just debts and funeral expenses be fully paid.

Item 2nd It is my wish that my wife receive from the use of the farm sufficient for her support in a good and comfortable manner and that she has the use of the farmed house for her life time

Item 3rd I give and bequeath to my youngest son Nathaniel Peter Corbett all my real estate, the farm on which I now reside situate in the township of Shalersville, County of Portage and State of Ohio containing twenty five acres and all the stock and farming utensils, Carriages and all the loose property about the farm upon condition that the said Nathaniel Peter Corbett pays or causes to be paid to his sister Mary Ann Baker the sum of fifty dollars within two years from the death of the said Nathaniel Corbett and to his sister Sarah Marilla Thompson the sum of

4-1. Nathaniel Corbett III's Will.

311

fifty dollars within three years from the death
of the said Nathaniel Corbett and his brother
Oliver Perry Corbett the sum of fifty dollars within
four years from the death of the said Nathaniel
Corbett and to his sister Caroline Amanda
Reaves the sum of fifty dollars within five years
from the death of the said Nathaniel Corbett and
the further sum of fifty dollars to his sister Laura
Osella McIntosh within six years from the death
of the said Nathaniel Corbett and the further
sum of fifty dollars to Celestia Matilda Clemmons
granddaughter of the said Nathaniel Peter Corbett within
seven years from the death of the said Nathaniel
Corbett and also the sum of fifty dollars each to
all of the above named commencing at Mary Ann
Been and paying fifty dollars a year until all
have received fifty dollars in addition to the first
fifty willed to them and in the same order.

Item 4 It is my wish that if the said Nathaniel Peter
Corbett should not live to be twenty one years of
age and should not have one male heir before
that time then the above described land is to go
to my son Oliver Perry Corbett or his heirs.

Item 5th It is my wish that when Nathaniel Peter Corbett
becomes of lawful age that he shall be administrator
and settle the remainder of my estate according to my
will.

Item 6th It is my wish that my daughter Laura Osella McIntosh
should have one cow, one bed with bedding, one table
one stand one sett of chairs and five dollars in
crockery.

Item 7th It is my wish that my son Nathaniel Peter Corbett
have one bed and bedding and that the balance of
the beds and bedding at the decease of my wife be
equally divided between my daughters and that my
son Nathaniel Peter Corbett should have the balance
of the household furniture including the cupboards
in the house.

Item 8th It is my wish that twenty dollars be sent to
Mary Ann Been ten dollars in the month of December
and ten dollars in the month of February not in
addition to her dower.

Item 9th I hereby appoint Vincent Turner to be Executor of
my last will and testament hereby authorizing

4-2. Nathaniel Corbett III's Will, continued.

312

and empowering him to compromise adjust, release and discharge in such manner as he may deem proper the debts and claims due me. I do also authorize and empower him if it shall become necessary in order to pay my debts to sell by private sale or in such manner as he may think proper all or any of my personal property.

Item 10th It is my wish that my son Nathaniel Peter Corbett remain with his Mother at home except when absent attending school.

In testimony whereof I have hereunto set my hand and seal this 19th day of November A.D. 1857.

Nathaniel Corbett (L.S.)

Signed and acknowledged by said Nathaniel Corbett as his last will and testament in our presence and signed by us in his presence.

Orson Judd.
Deloran Price.

The State of Ohio }
Portage County ss } We Orson Judd and Deloran Price being duly sworn in open Court this 17 day of Dec A.D. 1857, depose and say, That we were present at the execution of the last will and testament of Nathaniel Corbett hereto annexed; that we saw the said testator subscribe said will, and heard him publish and declare the same to be his last will and testament, and that the said testator, at the time of executing the same, was of full age, and of sound mind and memory and not under any restraint; and that we signed the same as witnesses at his request, and in his presence and in the presence of each other.

Orson Judd.
Deloran Price.

Attest D. Lyman Probate Judge.

Afterwards to wit on the 26 day of March A.D. 1858 Sarah Corbett widow of the said Nathaniel Corbett deceased, appeared in open Court and made her election to take the provision made for her under the last will and Testament in lieu of dower, under her signature

Sarah Corbett

Attest Darin Lyman, Probate Judge.

4-3. Nathaniel Corbett III's Will, continued.

5. 1860 U.S. Census listings for the William N. Thompson and Osman Calkins families.

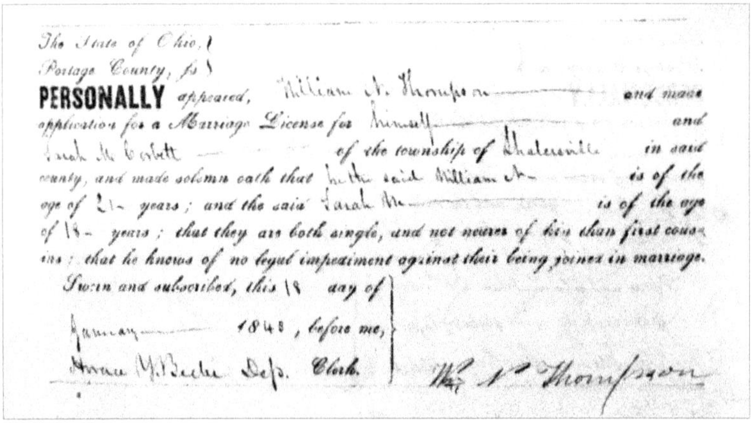

The State of Ohio,
Portage County, ss
PERSONALLY appeared, William N. Thompson and made application for a Marriage License for himself and Sarah M. Corbett of the township of Shalersville in said county, and made solemn oath that he the said William N. is of the age of 21 years; and the said Sarah M. is of the age of 18 years; that they are both single, and not nearer of kin than first cousins; that he knows of no legal impediment against their being joined in marriage.
Sworn and subscribed, this 18 day of January 1843, before me,
Horace Y. Beebe Dep. Clerk.
Wm N. Thompson

6. William N. Thompson & Sarah M. Corbett, Marriage Record.

Page No. 17

SCHEDULE 1.—Inhabitants in _Flushing_, in the County of _Genesee_, State of _Michigan_, enumerated by me on the _27_ day of _July_, 1870.

Post Office: _Flushing_   _John C. Howe,_ Ass't Marshal.

210

1	2	3	4	5	6	7	8	9	10	11	12	13	14	15	16	17	18	19	20	
		John	5	M	W				England	/	/									1
		James	3	M	W				"	/	/									2
		Lewis	M	W	W				Michigan	/	/	Pa								3
120	116	Fox Hiram	30	M	W	Farmer	800	357	New York									/		4
		Addis	25	F	W	Keeping House			"											5
		George	6	M	W	at School			"						/					6
		Lucina	2	F	W				Michigan											7
		Mary	30	F	W				"			Fra								8
121	117	Adams John	38	M	W	Farmer	800	250	New York			Feb						/		9
		Jemima	39	F	W	Keeping House			Canada	/	/	July								10
		Milligan James	19	M	W	Carpenter			"	/	/									11
122	118	Major Robert	32	M	W	Farmer	1400	250	Michigan									/		12
		Emily	30	F	W	Keeping House			"											13
		Frank	8	M	W	at school			"						/					14
		Scorpion	5	F	W	"			"						/					15
		Preston	1	M	W				"											16
123	119	Thompson William	56	M	W	Farmer	2800	500	New York									/		17
		Lizzie	40	F	W	Keeping House			Ohio											18
		Adelbert	23	M	W	Farm laborer			" "									/		19
		Sarah	22	F	W	at Home			" "											20
		Cornie	20	M	W	Farm laborer			" "											21
		William	19	M	W	at Home			" "											22
		Ella	7	F	W	at Home			Michigan						/					23
		Harriet	14	F	W	at school			"						/					24
		Rhoda	13	F	W	" "			"						/					25
		Delia	8	F	W	" "			"						/					26
		Emma	6	F	W	" "			"						/					27
		Willard	3	M	W				"											28
	124																			29
125	120	Moyer Adam	48	M	W	Farmer	2000	525	New York											30
		Eliza	30	F	W	Keeping House			"											31
		Gibson	5	M	W				Michigan											32
		Arthur	4	M	W				"											33
		Derby	12	M	W	Farm laborer			"						/					34
126	121	Pike Charles	40	M	W	Farmer	2000	450	New York									/		35
		Matilda	40	F	W	Keeping House			"											36
		Loretta	17	F	W	at Home			Michigan											37
		Isabel	15	F	W	"			"						/					38
		Kroly Matilda	6	F	W	at school			"						/					39
127	122	Daggett Henry	33	M	W	Farmer		280	New York											40

No. of Dwellings, _8_. No. of white females, _18_. No. of males, foreign born, _3_. _10,880_ _2375_   No. of Insane, _5_ _5_   _/_ _/_   _5_

" families, _7_. " colored males,   " " females,   " white males, _21_.   " Indian,

7.   1870 U.S. Census listing for William Thompson and family.

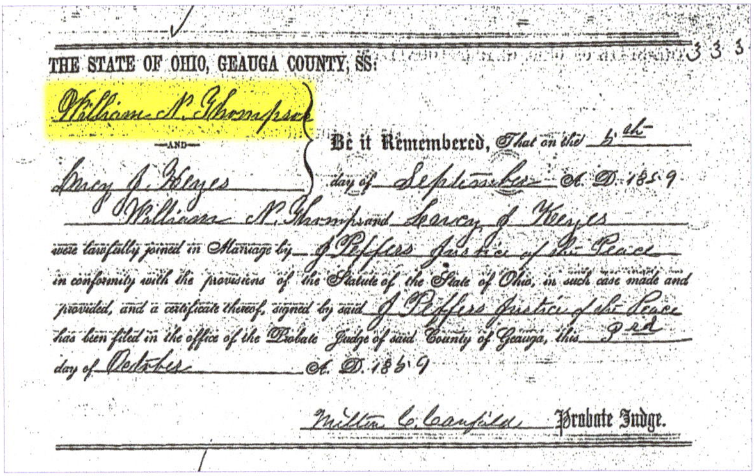

THE STATE OF OHIO, GEAUGA COUNTY, SS: 333

William N. Thompson

—AND—

Lucy J. Keyes

Be it Remembered, That on the 6th day of September A. D. 1859 William N. Thompson and Lucy J. Keyes were lawfully joined in Marriage by J. Peffers Justice of the Peace in conformity with the provisions of the Statute of the State of Ohio, in such case made and provided, and a certificate thereof, signed by said J. Peffers Justice of the Peace has been filed in the office of the Probate Judge of said County of Geauga, this 3rd day of October A. D. 1859

Milton C. Canfield Probate Judge.

8. William N. Thompson & Lucy Jane Keyes, Marriage Record.

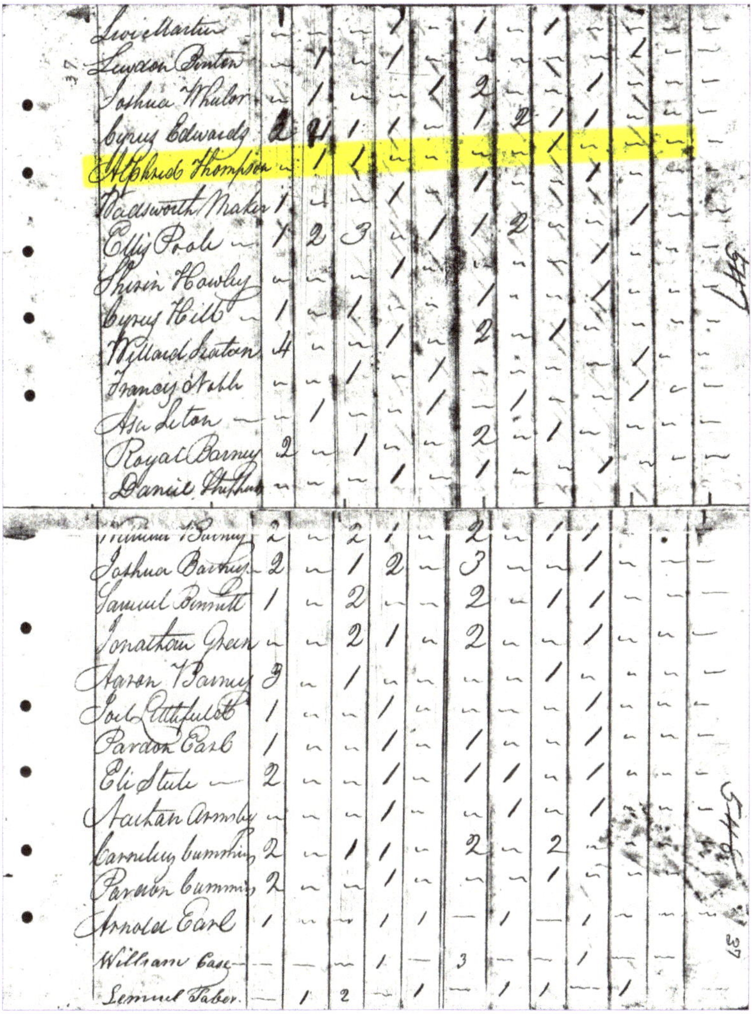

9. 1810 U.S. Census listing for Alfred Thompson.

10. 1820 U.S. Census listings for Needham Thompson and Alfred Thompson.

11. 1830 U.S. Census listings for Sally Thompson, Chroel Thompson, Levi Bemis, and Alfred Thompson.[87]

87   1830 U.S. Census, Ellisburg, Jefferson County, New York; Series: M19; Roll: 92; Page: 33; Family History Library Film: 0017152.

12. 1850 U.S. Census listing for Louden Thompson and family.

INDEX

www.ingramcontent.com/pod-product-compliance
Lightning Source LLC
Chambersburg PA
CBHW040829300326
41914CB00059B/1304